D1521816

The Sunny Side of Genealogy

A Humorous Collection
of Anecdotes, Poems,
Wills, Epitaphs, and
Other Miscellany From
Genealogy

Compiled by Fonda D. Baselt

Dedicated
To
My Family:

Walt, Jan, and Kendy

PREFACE

After several years of clipping and filing these splendid quotations, both in prose and verse, I decided to publish my collection for others who also enjoy the light and sunny side of genealogy.

The selections in this book have been gathered from numerous sources - genealogical quarterlies and newsletters, fellow researchers, historical magazines, and family histories.

I wish to thank those who so generously contributed material for this book and all of you who encouraged me to publish it.

THE SUNNY SIDE OF GENEALOGY

THE FAMILY TREE
by Carlton E. Blake

I think that I shall never see,
  The finish of a Family Tree.

As it forever seems to grow,
  From roots that started very low;

'Way back in ancient history times,
  In foreign lands and distant climes.

One seldom knows exactly when,
  The parents met and married then.

Nor when the twigs began to grow,
  With odd named children, row on row.

'Though a verse like this is made by me,
  And the end's in sight as you can see;

'Tis not the same with Family Trees,
  That grow and grow through centuries.

...

We find that a great part of the information we have ac-
quired is by looking up something and finding something
else on the way.

...

The past should be a guide post, not a hitching post.

THE SUNNY SIDE OF GENEALOGY

Genealogy is a lot like popcorn, once you get
started, it's hard to stop!

...

Epitaph:
Here lieth Richard Dent
in his last tenement. (1709)

...

It is a noble faculty of ours which enables us to
collect our thoughts, our sympathies and our happiness
with what is distant in place or times -- to hold
communion with our ancestors. We become their
contemporaries, live the lives they lived, endure what
they endured and partake of the rewards which they
enjoyed.   ---Daniel Webster

...

Birthday card:
> (1) I talked to Great Aunt Wilma the other day, and
> she said she still thinks you're the greatest
> thing that's ever happened to this family.
> (2) She also said Calvin Coolidge is President, the
> moon is made of cheese, and talking pictures
> will soon be the rage! Anyway, Happy Birthday!

...

Be the true man you seek.

If you would not be forgotten,
As soon as you are dead and rotten,
Either write things worthy of reading,
Or do things worth writing.
                    ---Benjamin Franklin, May 1738

...

Thrift is a wonderful virtue, especially in an ancestor.

...

COME WALK WITH US

Come walk with us,
Back through the vista of the years,
Which our ancestors knew.
We seek the trails which once they trod,
To find the spots where they once dwelt.
And while we search about our hearts,
Read weathered stones,
And turn musty pages of the past,
Their spirits come alive and walk with us.
We learn of them,
Their lives, their loves, their hates.
And with their knowledge,
Learn to understand ourselves,
For each of them has given to us a past.
We owe them this -
That they shall be remembered for that gift.
                    ---Fern Stokes Eller

...

If we aren't counting dollars, accomplishments,
calories or pounds, we're counting ancestors.

...

Epitaph:
            Here lies John Shore
            I say no more
            Who was alive
            In sixty five.

...

Success is relative --- the greater the success,
            the more the relatives.

...

Inscription in the Ancestral Hall at Wismar, Germany:
            "The Eternity that is gone
            and the Eternity to come
            Unite in your life.
            Your ancestors gave you
            Life and the power - to do.
            Your posterity will carry on
            Your desires and aspirations
            And you - between the two --
            Must cherish and increase
            What you have received --
            A worthy link in the unending chain"

...

4

A family historian who was writing his family history was dismayed to find that an ancestor had been publicly hanged. In a moment of inspiration he wrote "He died during a public ceremony, when the platform upon which he was standing collapsed beneath him".

Another family historian finding that a relative had been sent to the "chair" wrote "At the time of his death he occupied a chair of applied electricity at one of our most famous institutions".

...

Epitaph:
        On a Thursday she was born,
        On a Thursday made a bride,
        On a Thursday put to bed,
        On a Thursday broke her leg, and
        On a Thursday died.

...

The celebrated genealogist, tired of his many family trees, branched out.   ---Cryptoquip

...

Everyone has ancestors and it is only a question of going back far enough to find a good one.
        ---Howard Kenneth Nixon

...

Nostalgia is when you live in the past lane.

Thomas Overbury, a 17th century Englishman said, "The
man who has not anything to boast of but his illustrious
ancestors is like a potato---the only good belonging to
him is underground."

...

Epitaph:
    Here lies the body of L. Galdy, Esquire, who
    departed this life at Port Royal on the 22nd
    December 1739. Aged 30. He was born at Montpelier
    in France, but he left that Country for his Reli-
    gion, and came to settle in this Island, when he was
    swallowed up in the Great Earthquake in the year
    1692, and by the Providence of God was by another
    shock thrown into the Sea and miraculously saved by
    swimming until a boat took him up. He lived many
    years after in great reputation beloved by all that
    knew him, and much lamented at his death.

...

    Our chief want in genealogy is someone
    who will make us do what we can.

...

Every genealogist has the right to his or her own
opinions, but no genealogist should be wrong about
his facts.

...

SURNAMES FOR SALE

Surnames that I have in my ancestral line,
Four hundred now listed and all of them mine.
Are often most common like Jones or like Smith,
Like Johnson or Barber that we can live with;

But then there are others that lift, I suppose;
I've a Bliss and a Jasper, a Heaven and Rose.
And then there are some that just hit 'tween the eyes
And give you a shock, or a laugh, of surprise.

For years I have had one with name of John Death.
When I first had found him it near took my breath,
But then I thanked goodness I found such not often;
Then this week - believe it! - discovered Beth Coffin!

My wife I have teased about her pedigree,
That listed some queer ones as on my own tree,
For she has a Webb and a Cobb in her line.
Cobwebs in your ancestry surely is fine!

They say of our forebears we ought to be proud,
And not be supposing we're born 'neath a cloud,
But some of our names that we find make us wail
And tempted to offer some surnames for sale.

---Ora Barlow

...

Epitaph:
    Here lies an editor.

WILL OF JOHN GEORGE, LONDON 1791

"Seeing that I have had the misfortune to be married to
the aforesaid Elizabeth, who, ever since our union, has
tormented me in every possible way; that, not content
with making game of all my remonstrances, she has done
all she could to render my life miserable; that Heaven
seems to have sent her into the world solely to drive me
out of it; that the strength of Samson, the genius of
Homer, the prudence of Augustus, the skill of Pyrrhus,
the patience of Job, the philosophy of Socrates, the
subtlety of Hannibal, the vigilance of Hermogenes, would
not suffice to subdue the perversity of her character;
that no power on earth can change her, seeing we have
lived apart during the last eight years, and that the
only result has been the ruin of my son, whom she has
corrupted and estranged from me; weighing maturely and
seriously all these considerations, I have bequeathed,
and I bequeath, to my said wife Elizabeth, the sum of
one shilling, to be paid unto her within six months of
my death."

...

When we were young, we did not ask questions;
Now that we're old, there's no one to answer them.

...

Why Is It?
   Just as you are hot on the trail of an ancestor,
   it's always time for the library to close?

8

RESEARCH IN RHYME

I started out calmly tracing my tree
To find, if I could, the makings of me.
And all that I had was great grandfather's name,
Not knowing his wife or from which way he came.

I chased him across a long line of states,
And came up with pages and pages of dates.
When all put together it made me forlorn,
I'd proved poor great grandpa had never been born.

One day I was sure the truth I had found,
Determined to turn this whole thing upside down.
I looked up the records of one Uncle John,
But found the old man to be younger than son.

Then when my hopes were fast growing dim,
I came across records that must have been him.
The facts I collected then made me quite sad,
Dear old Great Grandfather was never a dad.

I think maybe someone is pulling my leg,
I'm not at all sure I wasn't hatched from an egg.
After hundreds of dollars I've spent on my tree,
I can't help but wonder if I'm really me.
                                        ---Mrs Chas. Dean

                    . . .

May all your ancestors be like vegetables in the fall --
turnip!!

"In our family", the little girl told her teacher,
"everybody married relatives. My father married my
mother, my uncle married my aunt, and just the other day
I found out that my grandfather married my grandmother".

. . .

We inherit nothing truly, but what our actions make us
worthy of.   ---George Chapman

. . .

HAVE PRIDE IN HUMBLE ANCESTRY

It is the humble people I seek,
The salt of the earth so to speak,
The ones that cleared the land,
And sowed the grain with bare hand.

They are the ones I like to meet
When traveling the genealogy street,
It's for pride in them I play the game
To preserve for posterity their name.

Those who pursue it in hopes of glory,
Of finding heros and royal story,
In disappointment must not frown,
When learning their ancestor is wearing
A margarine crown.
                                    ---Guylia McCoy

. . .

Wilbur: "I have to borrow this picture of you and
          Dad. Okay, Mom? I'll need this picture
          of Grandma and Grandpa, too. Could I
          borrow some tracing paper?"

Mom: "Just what are you doing, Wilbur?"

Wilbur: "Tracing my ancestry!"

                    • • •

When a society or a civilization perishes, one condition
can always be found; they forgot where they came from.
                                    ---Carl Sandburg
                    • • •

        Epitaph:
              'Twas by a fall I caught my death;
              No man can tell his time or breath.
              I might have died as soon as then
              If I had had physician men.

                    • • •

A sign on the door in plain view as you enter the office
of the County Clerk of Macon County, Bill Tangney,
reads: "Have you hugged your County Clerk lately?"

                    • • •

It takes an endless amount of history to make even a
little tradition.   ---Henry James

IF

If you could see your ancestors
All standing in a row,
Would you be proud of them?
Or don't you really know?
Some mighty strange discoveries are made
In climbing family trees,
And some of them, you know
Might not particularly please

If you could see your ancestors
All standing in a row
There might be some of them
You wouldn't care to know.
But here is another question
That requires a different view.
If you could meet your ancestors,
What would they think of you?"
                              ---Mable Baker

...

(about wills)
The tongues of dying men
Enforce attention like deep harmony...
                              ---Shakespeare

...

I don't know who my grandfather was, I am much more
concerned to know what his grandson will be.
                              ---Abraham Lincoln

12

If one's mother runs off with a traveling salesman,
    it is considered scandalous.
But if one's great-great-grandmother did so,
    ah, that's romance!

...

THE FAMILY TREE
by Jean E. Sailer

Tell me, have you ever seen
    An elm branch on an evergreen?
When oak and birch grow close and touch
    Does this affect their seedlings much?
If, indeed, a freak should sprout
    The whispering pines would talk, no doubt.

Perhaps you think there'll never be
    That crazy kind of mixed up tree;
But you are wrong. I tell no lie!
    Great branches reaching to the sky
Have different leaves...I guarantee
    They're growing on a family tree.

So if your roots have crossed the seas
    With mixed-up nationalities,
Don't be disturbed...new roots will take,
    Then when you give your tree a shake
You'll realize the whole darn clan
    Is what we call American!

...

13

THE LAWS OF GENEALOGY

The document containing evidence of the missing link in your research invariably will be lost due to fire, flood, or war.

The keeper of the vital records you need will just have been insulted by another genealogist.

Your great, great, grandfather's obituary states that he died, leaving no issue of record.

The town clerk you wrote to in desperation, and finally convinced to give you the information you need, can't write legibly, and doesn't have a copying machine.

The will you need is in the safe on board the "Titanic".

The spelling of your European ancestor's name bears no relationship to its current spelling or pronunciation.

That ancient photograph of four relatives, one of whom is your progenitor, carries the names of the other three.

Copies of old newspapers have holes which occur only on last names.

No one in your family tree ever did anything noteworthy, always rented property, was never sued, and was never named in wills.

cont'd

14

cont'd

You learned that great aunt Matilda's executor just sold her life's collection of family genealogical materials to a flea market dealer "somewhere in New York City".

Yours is the ONLY last name not found among the three billion in the world-famous Mormon archives in Salt Lake City.

Ink fades and paper deteriorates at a rate inversely proportional to the value of the data recorded.

The 37-volume, sixteen-thousand-page history of your county of origin isn't indexed.

The critical link in your family tree is named "Smith".
---Author Unknown

...

Epitaph:
There lies the body of John Smith.
Had he lived till he got ashore,
he would have been buried here.

...

Mrs. Beth A. Baer, a blind woman, wrote out her will with a pen that ran out of ink. Handwriting expert, Clark Sellers, was able to make out the words from the indentations left on the paper by the pen.

Some men by ancestry are only the shadow of a mighty
name.   ---Lucan

...

ALL I WANT FOR CHRISTMAS

Dear Santa: Don't bring me new dishes;
I don't need a new kind of game.
Genealogists have peculiar wishes;
For Christmas I just want a surname.

A new washing machine would be great,
But it's not the desire of my life.
I've just found an ancestor's birth date;
What I need now is the name of his wife.

My heart doesn't yearn for a ring
That would put a real diamond to shame.
What I want is a much cheaper thing:
Please give me Mary's last name.

To see my heart singing with joy,
Don't bring me a red leather suitcase.
Bring me a genealogist's toy:
A surname, with dates and a place.
                                      ---Author unknown

...

He may make a will upon his nail for anything he has to
give.   ---Old Proverb

THE GENEALOGIST'S PSALM
by Wildamae Brestal

Genealogy is my pastime, I shall not stray;
It maketh me to lie down and examine half-buried
                                    tombstones.
It leadeth me into still Court Houses,
    it restoreth my ancestral knowledge.
It leadeth me in paths of census records and ships'
                                    passengers lists
    for my surname's sake.

Yea, though I walk through the shadows of research
                        libraries and microfilm readers,
    I shall fear no discouragement;
for a strong urge is within me;
    the curiosity and motivation
    they comforteth me.

It demandeth preparation of storage space for the
                    acquisition of countless documents;
it anointest my head with burning midnight oil,
    my family group sheets runneth over.
Surely birth, marriage and death dates shall follow me
                            all the days of my life;
and I shall dwell in the house of a family-history
                                    seeker
    for ever.

                        ...

Fame is chiefly a matter of dying at the right moment.

17

PEDIGREE

His father was a Jones of the Joneses of Old Whoop,
Hezekiah Jones was Captain of a famous fighting sloop,
Azariah Jones commanded at the battle of Great Neck.
In the dark old days of trouble, all the Jones were on
    deck.

Down thru noble lines he came, honors written o'er his
    name.
Many a man would give a fortune for the lineage he can
    claim.

His mother was a Brown of Massachusetts Browns,
Who were citizens of Plymouth and those other good old
    towns,
When the savages shot arrows through the Puritans' tall
    hats,
And they soused the wicked witches, out of sight, in
    boiling vats.

On his mother's side, there was power, honor, and pride.
That the Browns made up a splendid stock, has never
    been denied.

His father was a sturdy Jones, his mother was a Brown.
He told me of the lines thru which his blood had
    trickled down.
His pedigree would gladden many a longing millionaire,
Last night as I sat silent while he deftly cut my
    hair.

---Author Unknown

18

Whenever there's a will, you'll see an heir loom.

...

"My family's ancestry is very old", said one club member trying to impress the group. "We can be traced back to the early kings of Europe." Then, turning to a lady sitting nearby, she asked, "And how old is your family, my dear?"

"I really don't know," replied the lady with a sweet smile. "All our family records were lost in the great flood."

...

GENEALOGY

Genealogy begins as an interest,
Becomes a hobby;
Continues as an avocation,
Takes over as an obsession,
And in its last stages,
Is an incurable disease.

...

Epitaph:
    Here lies Richard Fothergill who met a violent
    death. He was shot by a colt's revolver, old
    kind, brass mounted, and of such is the kingdom
    of heaven.

...

19

GRANDMA'S GENEALOGY
by Virginia R. Kennedy

Remember, as a little child,
You sat on Grandma's knee
And listened while she told you tales
About the family.

She told about the folks she knew
And those she'd heard about.
So many names, she mentioned,
It was hard to sort them out.

You got them pictured, one by one;
You had their names to guide you,
And now you'd give a million
Just to have them here beside you.

Grandma isn't here today;
She gave up on life's game.
Oh! How you wish she'd left a list
Of each and every name.

Dear Friends, pray sit thee down today
And write your family tree.
Make notes of those you know today
And those of memory.

Remember, there may come a day
YOUR grandchild on YOUR knee
Will look up at you longingly
And say, "Grandma, who are we?"

20

Old genealogists never die,
They just lose their census.

...

A Will:
  J. WITHIPOL, of Walthamstow, left his landed
  estates to his wife, "trusting, yea, I may say,
  as I think, assuring myself, that she will marry
  no man, for fear to meet with so evil a husband
  as I have been to her."

...

Epitaph:
  This is the sweetest sight I've seen in my life,
  For it raises my flowers and covers my wife.

...

There's one in every family,
Who catalogues and makes collections
Of family feats, noble deeds,
And ancestorial recollections.
At last, when all the data's in,
The clan has got its pedigree
(Never mentioning Great Uncle Pete...
They hanged him from an old oak tree.)
                 ---Colleen Stanley Bare

...

Good wine needs no vine. --- French proverb

Truth sits upon the lips of dying men.
                    ---Matthew Arnold

...

The cheapest way to have your family tree traced is to
run for public office.

...

RESEARCH is the process of going up alleys to see if
they're blind.   ---Reader's Digest

...

To forget one's ancestors is to be a brook without a
source, a tree without a root.   ---Chinese proverb

...

There is a destiny that makes us brothers:
    None goes his way alone:
All that we send into the lives of others
    Comes back into our own.
                    ---Edwin Markham

...

Cartoon:
    One chicken to another: "Hey, I traced my family
    tree, but along came Colonel Sanders, now
    there's only me!"

22

THE FAMILY GENEALOGY
by Donald Lines Jacobus

Compendium of dullness, in your pages
    Name crowds on name; the humble and the great
Each in few lines receives his equal wages,
    And headstrong passions crumble to a date.
Here are the founders of a mighty nation;
    Here are the pioneers who won the soil,
As generation followed generation,
    With ax and plough and with back-breaking toil.
Here are the women of a hardy people,
    Weakness and doubt yielding to faith held fast,
They pulled up stakes; eyes lifted to the steeple;
    Farewells to home; the new homes gained at last:
Here are the hints of buried new romances,
    The broken families, and the too young dead:
The autumn frolics and the village dances;
    Roll of recruiting drums, the soldier's tread
And here are darker things, now long forgotten;
    The unwed mothers; the deserted wives;
Misdeeds of rogues far better unbegotten;
    Heartbreak and self-destruction; ruined lives.
All this and far far more is in these pages
    If we might clothe with flesh the lifeless names,
Parade the knaves, the saints, the fools, the sages,
    and resurrect their obloquies and fames.
Their names, their dates, are entered in a column,
    The unjust here embalmed beside the just;
And in the pages of this dusty volume,
    A second time they moulder in the dust.

...

We have to be learning ourselves in order to explain to others.

...

Learning to do genealogy is like learning to walk.
It's easy if you learn one step at a time.

...

It is of no consequence of what parents a man is born,
so he be a man of merit.   ---Horace

...

Spring is sprung, grass is riss,
I wonder where my great-grandpa is!

...

For books are more than books, they are the life,
    the very heart and core of ages past;
The reason why men lived, and worked, and died,
    the essence and quintessence of their lives.
                        ---James Russell Lowell

...

Epitaph:
    Ann Jennings
    Some have children, some have none
    Here lies the mother of twenty-one.

24

History repeats itself.
That's one of the things wrong with history.

...

We relish news of our heroes, forgetting that we are
extraordinary to somebody, too.   ---Helen Hayes

...

THE MAN NEXT DOOR - by Burton Hillis
Nell Moore wonders if the colonists who named their
children for virtues like Charity, Patience, and
Prudence would choose names like Assertiveness,
Self-Actualization, and Positive Thinking if they
were alive today.

...

Nostalgia is a file that removes the rough edges from
the good old days.   ---Doug Larson

...

Bumpersticker:
          We're traveling on our kids' inheritance.

...

A Will:
    "Being of sound mind, I spent every cent when I
    was alive".

25

It is indeed desirable to be well descended, but the glory belongs to our ancestors.   ---Plutarch

•••

The past at least is secure.---Daniel Webster

•••

There is no cure for birth and death save to enjoy the interval.   ---Santayana

•••

A BETTER WAY

There is no return
     to the things we did
     in the hours of yesterday.
But we can go forward
     to better things
     and do them a better way.
We cannot retrace
     the steps we have made
     Nor call back
     the words we said.
No, we cannot do
     things over again---
     But we can do better instead.
          ---Everett Wentworth Hill

•••

THE FORMULA
by Rodney A. Biagioni

1 tsp of grandma's eyes,
2 shakes of Uncle Fred's blond hair
A pinch of great grandpa's smile
As much love as you can give
Mix well and let rise with time.

...

Birthday card:
    (1) You've made this family what it is today!
    (2) But since it's your Birthday, we'll forgive you.
        Happy Day!

...

Epitaph in Thurmont, VA:
        Here lies an atheist;
        All dressed up and no place to go.

...

There are only two lasting bequests we can hope to give
our children: One of these is roots, the other, wings.
                        ---Hodding Carter

...

Epitaph:
        This corpse is Phoebe Thorp's.

...

27

What the future has in store for you depends largely on what you place in store for the future.

         ...

He who fails to commemorate the deeds of his ancestors, deserves to be forgotten, himself.

         ...

      Wrinkles are hereditary.
  Parents get them from their children.

         ...

Overheard at a genealogical society meeting:
    "Joan is a sweet gal, but she needs some help with
    her genealogy. She thinks that oak in the backyard
    is her family tree."

Also overheard:
    Her mother told her that Time is Relative and now
    she is looking for her ancestor named Time.

         ...

  Epitaph:
      Here lies one Box within another;
          The one of wood
          Was very good;
      We cannot say so much for t' other.
         ...

BEATITUDES OF A FAMILY GENEALOGIST
by Wilma Mauk

Blessed are the great-grandfathers, who saved
  embarkation and citizenship papers, for they tell
  WHEN they came.

Blessed are the great-grandmothers, who hoarded
  newspaper clippings and old letters, for they tell
  the STORY of their time.

Blessed are the grandfathers, who filed every legal
  document, for these provide the PROOF.

Blessed are the grandmothers, who preserved family
  Bibles and diaries, for these are our HERITAGE.

Blessed are fathers, who elect officials that answer
  letters of inquiry, for--to some--the ONLY LINK to
  the past.

Blessed are mothers, who relate family TRADITIONS and
  LEGENDS to the family, for one of her children will
  surely remember.

Blessed are relatives, who fill in family sheets with
  extra data, for to them we owe our FAMILY HISTORY.

Blessed is any family, whose members strive for the
  PRESERVATION of RECORDS, for this is a labor of
  love.

cont'd

cont'd

Blessed are the children who will never say,
    "Grandma, you told that old story twice today".

...

Everyone has something ancestral, even if it is nothing
more than a disease.   ---Ed Howe

...

    If the past was a mold for the present,
    Let the present be a mold for the future.

...

OCUPSYSHUN - Cencus Taker:
        "I am a cencus takers for the city of
    Bufflow. Our City has groan very fast in resent
    years & now in 1865, it has become a hard & time
    consuming job to count all the peephill. There
    are not many that con do this werk, as it is
    nesessarie to have an ejucashun, wich a lot of
    pursons still do not have. Anuther atribeart
    needed for this job is god spelling, for meny of
    the pephill to be counted can hardle speek
    inglish, let alon spel there names!"

...

"Heritage of the past is the seed that brings forth the
harvest of the future."   (National Archives Building)

THE OLD HOME PLACE
by Grace Brown Wagner

The town is very much the same,
With some changes, that is true,
But there are no changes in the handshakes,
With the people I once knew.

Truer Friendships linger there,
With my friends out in the West,
And the people there will always be,
The ones I love the best.

The prairie holds a beauty,
That is easy for me to see,
For it was my childhood home,
And is still a part of me.

The old home place still stands,
Defiant until the last,
Its weather beaten shingles,
Just a landmark of the past.

Many long years have passed,
And my longing ends in despair,
For I know I am homesick,
For a home - a home that isn't there.

. . .

The family you come from isn't as important as the
family you're going to have.

No man knows himself unless he knows his ancestors;
No nation knows itself unless it knows its past.
                              ---Ben Ames Williams

                          •••

                      ANCESTORS
                  by GeorgeAnne Taylor

      I'm trying hard and hope to find
      Some records that were left behind
      By people, who I think might be
      Branches of my Family Tree.

      For some of them I've searched for years;
      Searched first with joy and then with fears
      But always hoping for a clue
      To help me start my search anew.

      Perhaps some day I'll take a look
      And find the past is like a book
      That's filled with names, which, if I had 'em
      I'd trace my lineage back to Adam.

                          •••

Marriage Record in Shelby Co., Tenn:
      Josiah Nolly to Manervy Owen, Nov. 28, 1848. (Note
      on back of marriage license reads: "Returned not
      executed. Lady hid under bed. Jan. 15, 1849.")

                          •••

Have pride in the past, faith in the future.

...

Remember the days of old; consider the generations long past. Ask your father and he will tell you, your elders, and they will explain to you.

---Deuteronomy 32:7

...

We adore titles and heredities in our hearts,
and ridicule them with our mouths.
---Mark Twain

...

Epitaph:
    In a French cemetery there are the following concise inscriptions on one tombstone. The epitaph is for a husband and wife:

I am anxiously	Here I am!
expecting you.	A.D. 1827
A.D. 1827	

...

The real purpose of our existence is not to make a living, but to make a life---a worthy, well-rounded, useful life.

...

33

THE PUZZLED CENSUS-TAKER
by John G. Saxe

"Got any boys?" the marshal said
To a lady from over the Rhine;
And the lady shook her flaxen head,
And civilly answered "Nein".

"Got any girls?" the marshal said
To the lady from over the Rhine;
And again the lady shook her head,
And civilly answered, "Nein".

"But some are dead?" the marshal said
To the lady from over the Rhine;
And again the lady shook her head,
And civilly answered, "Nein".

"Husband, of course," the marshal said
To the lady from over the Rhine;
And again she shook her flaxen head,
And civilly answered, "Nein".

"The devil you have." the marshal said
To the lady from over the Rhine;
And again she shook her flaxen head,
And civilly answered, "Nein".

"Now, what do you mean by shaking your head,
And always answering 'Nein'?"
"Ich kann nicht Englisch" civilly said
The lady from over the Rhine.

34

A Will of 1804:
> Maybe I am not worth a groat,
> But should I die worth something more,
> I leave it all, with my old coat,
> And all my manuscripts in store,
> To those who will the goodness have
> To cause my poor remains to rest
> Within a fitting shell and grave:
> This is the will of Joshua West.

...

If you cannot get rid of the family skeleton, you may as well make it dance.   ---George Bernard Shaw

...

> Epitaph for a Waiter:
> By and by
> God caught his eye.

...

Good blood, descent from the great and good, is a high honor and privilege. He that lives worthily of it is deserving of the highest esteem; he that does not, of the deeper disgrace.   ---Colton

...

Advice to persons about to write history...DON'T.
...

THE SUNNY SIDE OF GENEALOGY

People will not look forward to posterity who never look
backward to their ancestors.   ---Edmund Burke

•••

   Epitaph for Peter Robinson...
          Here lies the preacher, judge, and poet, Peter
          Who broke the laws of God, and man, and metre.
                              ---Lord Jeffrey

•••

Let each one who bears the Cary name
Remember whence his shield and motto came;
All that the family have by valor gained,
Must by the sons be valiantly maintained.
Then take the shield; go forward to the fight;
Guard well the roses; may their silvery light
 Shine on brave deed performed for truth and right.
                         ---"Cary-Estes Genealogy"

•••

   Epitaph
          Here lies one blown out of breath,
          Who lived a merry life, and died a Merideth.

•••

   Epitaph for a Dentist:
          Stranger!
          Approach this spot with gravity!
          John Brown is filling his last cavity.

ANCESTRY
by Josephine Powell Segal

When first I began my search to see
What I could learn of my Ancestry,
They seemed to me so far away
As if they had lived in Caesar's day;
But my interest grew and great pains I took
To find my own in each history's book.
As their names and deeds came to the light
The ages vanished like mists of the night;
As they came so near I seemed to see
My beloved, forgotten Ancestry.

Now I have them with me with their powdered
 hair,
Wearing beruffled shirts, so debonair;
Their pleated coats and flowered vests,
The signet rings with their jeweled crests;
The satin breeches that fit so tight,
Begemmed knee clasps shining bright;
Long silk stocking and polished shoe
With their buckles of brightened silver, too;
They seem so near and dear to me,
My new found friends, my Ancestry.
"That like thine elders so thou mightest behold
Thy children many, famous, stout and bold."

. . .

HEREDITY: Something you believe in when your child's
report card is all A's.

37

THE BORN LOSER - by Art Sansom

> (1) "This is the Genealogy Department of the Public
> Library, Mr. Thornapple..."

> (2) "We have started to trace your family roots and
> have made a discovery concerning your late
> grandfather..."
>
> "Yes? Yes?"

> (3) "You are responsible for his accrued fines of
> $1,112.29!"

•••

> Epitaph:
> Here lies the body of Henry Round
> Who went to sea and never was found.

•••

Will of London Attorney, Smithers:
As to all my worldly goods now, or to be, in store,
I give to my beloved wife, and hers for evermore.
I give all freely, I no limit fix:
This is my will, and she's executrix.

•••

> Graves are but the footprints
> of the angel of eternal life.

38

Epitaph:
>Here lies John Hill, a man of skill,
>His age was five times ten,
>He ne'er did good, nor ever would,
>Had he lived as long again.

...

Epitaph:
>Here lies the body of Thomas Vernon,
>The only surviving son of Admiral Vernon.

...

Counting time is not as important as making time count.

...

THE CENSUS

Census Taker: "Good morning, madam, I'm taking the census".

Old Lady: "The what?"

Census Taker: "The c-e-n-s-u-s!"

Old Lady: "For lan sakes! what with tramps takin' everythin' they kin lay their han's on, young folks takin' fotygrafs of ye without so much as askin', an' impudent fellows comin' roun' as wants ter take yer senses, pretty soon there won't be nothin' left ter take, I'm thinkin'."
>---1890 Harper's Weekly.

39

Those only deserve to be remembered by posterity who
treasure up a history of their ancestors.

---Edmund Burke

...

A 1789 RHYMING WILL

I give and bequeath,
When I'm laid underneath,
To my two loving sisters most dear,
The whole of my store,
Were it twice as much more,
Which God's goodness has given me here.

And that none may prevent
This my will and intent,
Or occasion the least of law-racket,
With a solemn appeal
I confirm, sign, and seal
 This the true act and deed of Will Jacket.

...

When you know all the answers, you haven't asked the
right questions.

...

Epitaph for a hunter...
A bird, a man, a loaded gun,
No bird, dead man, thy will be done.

THE GENEALOGY BUG
by Marcy Hagel

You follow many dead end trails
As you search through dusty files,
You weaken your eyes with microfilm
And travel for miles and miles,
You rummage through church records
And interview over the phone,
You look for Grandma's marriage
And find she had children alone,
You write many unanswered letters
To people across the sea,
You find your Great Uncle Zanzibar
Was hung for shooting Aunt Bea,
You ignore your dust and dishes,
You never vacuum the rug,
You've caught a disease that has no cure,
You have the genealogy bug.

• • •

Epitaph:
        Here lies John Bun,
        He was killed by a gun,
        His name was not Bun, but Wood,
        But Wood would not rhyme with gun,
        But Bun would.

• • •

Every man's work is a portrait of himself.

41

THE MAN NEXT DOOR - by Burton Hillis
    Judy was surprised to hear Grandma Hillis say that
    most of her schoolmates never went beyond eighth
    grade. "Of course, in those days," she explained,
    "there were 60 fewer years of history to learn."

                        • • •

              Epitaph At Leeds...
                    Here lies my wife,
                    Here lies she;
                    Hallelujah!
                    Hallelujee!

                        • • •

To be ignorant of what happened before you were born is
to be ever a child. For what is man's lifetime unless
the memory of past events is woven with those of earlier
times.   ---Cicero

                        • • •

"CENSUS - An authentik register or enumeration of the
inhabitants of a country made bi publik authority."

                        • • •

Why Is It?
    The blot on the page of the census covers your
    grandmother's birthdate?
                        • • •

A WHIMSICAL WILL OF 1737

The fifth day of May,
    Being airy and gay,
And to hyp not inclined,
    But of vigorous mind,
And my body in health,
    I'll dispose o' my wealth,
And all I'm to leave
    On this side the grave,
To some one or other,
    And I think to my brother.
Because I foresaw
    That my brothers-in-law,
If I did not take care,
    Would come in for their share,
Which I nowise intended,
    Till their manners are mended;
And o't, God knows, there's no sign;
    I do therefore enjoin,
And do strictly command,
    Of which witness my hand,
That nought I have got
    Be brought into hotch-pot;
But I give and devise,
    As much as in me lies,
To the son of my mother,
    My own dear brother,
To have and to hold,
    All my silver and gold,
As the affectionate pledges
    Of his brother --- John Hedges

43

(About Wills)
"Voice of the dead not lost,
But speaking from Death's frost,
Like fiery tongues at Pentecost."
                        ---Longfellow

...

No one is ever too old to learn, but many people keep
putting it off.

...

BLONDIE - by Young & Drake

Blondie: "How do you like the shirt I bought you?
        It has our royal family crest over the
        pocket."
Dagwood: "Since when do we have a royal family
        crest?"
Blondie: "Since I bought you that shirt."

...

Birthday card:
        (1) Happy Birthday!
            Who says our family is worthless!?
        (2) Have you priced nuts lately?

...

The rich never have to seek out their relatives.

44

Genealogy is like love!
It's best when shared with another.

...

Little drops of water, little grains of sand,
Make the mighty ocean and the pleasant land.
So the little minutes, humble though they be,
Make the mighty ages of eternity.
---Julia Fletcher Carney

...

GENEALOGY: Tracing yourself back to people better than
you are.   ---John Garland Pollard

...

What the future has in store for you depends largely on
what you place in store for the future.

...

The art of biography
Is different from geography.
Geography is about maps,
But biography is about chaps.
---Edmund Clerihew Bentley

...

History is the essence of innumerable biographies.

45

Facts are stubborn things.

...

Civilization begins with order, grows with liberty, and dies in chaos.   ---Will Durant

...

Praise is the shipwreck of historians.

...

NO SKELETONS IN OUR CLOSETS

No family skeletons,
Naked or gowned,
In our closets ever
Will rattle around.

But don't be too hasty,
Too quick to presume.
It's not lack of scandals,
It's lack of room.
                ---Richard Armour

...

Epitaph:
    Here lies one whose name was writ in water.

...

Epitaph:
    In loving memory of Jan Bent
    Kicked up her heels
    And away she went.

                    •••

IN ANOTHER WILL:
    The husband left to his widow the sum of five
    hundred guineas; but added the clause that she was
    only to come into the enjoyment of it after her
    death, "in order," said this considerate (or perhaps
    outraged) husband, "that she may be buried suitably
    as my widow".

                    •••

Epitaph:
    Gone To See For Myself.

                    •••

You spend an eternity looking for your grandmother's
maiden name, and when you find it, your mother tells you
she already knew that but you had never asked her.

                    •••

Epitaph:
    I Expected This,
    But Not So Soon.
                •••

47

REGARDING FATHER'S WILL

Of all my father's family
I like myself the best.
And if I am provided for,
The Devil take the rest.

...

None of us can boast about the morality of our
ancestors. The records do not show that Adam and Eve
were married.

...

PATRICK HENRY'S WILL:

Patrick Henry immortalized the words "Give me
liberty or give me death". In his will he
stipulated that his wife would have all his property
only so long as she remained unmarried. Apparently
Mrs. Henry felt as strongly about liberty as her
husband had. She did remarry, and fought for her
legal share of the estate in court.

...

Heinrich Heine left his wife all his assets, with one
condition--that she remarry. "Because then there will
be at least one man to regret my death."

...

48

THE GENEALOGY BUG
by Alice Mickey Weddle

Our world is a quiet, peaceful place
We go along at a smooth, even pace;
Until that bug, "Genealogy" bites
Then all is changed, both days and nights.

We search and research each nook and cranny
To find all we can about Gramp and Granny,
Dad and Mom, Uncles and Cousins
We quiz them all, dozens and dozens.

In books we read, in records we search
In old courthouses and in the church;
We hope to find a great, or a great great
Where they lived, why and how they rate.

With pleasure our records we compile
Each one we add brings a smile;
We are inspired, life is much brighter
That bug, "Genealogy" is a real biter.

...

The fence around a cemetery is foolish, for those inside
can't get out and those outside don't want to get in.

...

She's descended from a long line her mother listened to.
---Gypsy Rose Lee

49

One doctor tells his patients: "Get plenty of exercise, stay away from alcohol and cigarettes, and pray that you've picked the right ancestors!"

...

1880 Epitaph in Nantucket, Mass:
                Under the sod and under the trees
                Lies the body of Jonathan Pease:
                He is not here, there's only the pod
                Pease shelled out and went to God.

...

Youth is a blunder; manhood a struggle; old age a regret.   ---Benjamin Disraelie 1804-1881

...

One of the stipulations in the will of Edwin Orlando Swain was that all his creditors be paid except the landlord.

...

If you write about things, add the
people you know best and discover
your roots. Even if they are new roots,
fresh roots, they are better than no roots.
                        ---Isaac B. Sikger

...

50

The only thing some people do is grow older.

•••

Epitaph:
     Here lies the body of
       Mary Ann Lowder
     She burst while drinking
       A seidlitz powder:
     Called from this world
       To her heavenly rest:
     She drank it and she effervesced.

•••

It is worthwhile for anyone to have behind him a few generations of honest, hard working ancestry.
                     ---John Phillip Marquand

•••

Epitaph in Gerard, PA:
     In memory of
     Ellen Shannon
     Aged 26 years
     Who was fatally burned
     March 21st, 1870
     By the explosion of a lamp
     Filled with R.E. Danforth's
     Non-Explosive Burning Fluid.

•••

51

Epitaph:
Here lies a father of 29
There would have been more
But he didn't have time.

...

"Let every man honor and love the land of his birth and
the race from which he springs and keep their memory
green. It is a pious and honorable duty..."

---Henry Cabot Lodge

...

GOLD ATTRACTS GOLD - 1700

An old bachelor of fortune, finding himself near his
end, sent for his notary and made his will, leaving all
his fortune to one of his friends.

"How is this," said the notary, "you leave all you
possess to a stranger when you have a nephew?"

"My nephew!" exclaimed the old man furiously, "My
nephew! A good-for-nothing spendthrift, who hasn't a
penny, and has disobeyed me in everything."

"O dear no, that is quite a mistake," said the
notary, "since you last saw him two years ago he has
made a large fortune."

"What, is that true?" answered the bachelor, "He is
rich? That is quite another thing; in that case I make
him absolutely my heir."

...

A man had a legacy left him; it was hampered by an unfortunate condition, which he hastened to announce to a sympathising friend. The sum was L2000, but half of it, according to the testator's wishes, was to be placed in his coffin and buried with him.

The sympathiser was equal to the occasion. "Where is the money now?" he asked, and was told, "In the bank."

"All right," he said; "you write a cheque for L1000, and put it in the old gentleman's coffin, drawn to order."

...

Epitaph in Plymouth, England:
Here lies as silent clay
Miss Arabella Young
Who on the 21st of May 1771
Began to hold her tongue.

...

IN THE NEWS:
Moses Alexander, aged 93, to Mrs. Frances Tompkins, aged 105. They were married in Bath, Steuben Co., NY, June 11, 1831. They were both taken out of bed dead the following morning.

...

You can't choose your ancestors, but that's fair enough. They probably wouldn't have chosen you.

THE ABC's OF GENEALOGICAL RESEARCH

A Archives . Ancestor
   Charts

B Bibles . Birth Records
   . Biographies

C Courthouses . Churches

D Diaries . Deeds

E Evidence Evaluation

F Family . Funerals

G Grants . Gravestones

H Heraldry . Hospitals

I Interviews

J Journeys . Join a
   Genealogical Society

K Kinfolks

L Libraries . Land
   Records

M Military Records .
   Marriages

N Naturalizations .
   Newspapers

O Obituaries . Organiza-
   tions

P Pension Papers .
   Passenger Lists

Q Queries. Quarterlies

R Reunions

S School Records . State
   Records

T Tax Lists . Tradition

U U.S. Census

V Vital Records . Visits

W Wills . Writing
   Letters

X Xeroxing

Y Yearbooks

Z Zodiac Signs

It is indeed a desirable thing to be well descended,
but the glory belongs to our ancestors.

•••

A man who owns land and lives on it eventually creates
his own self-portrait in the fields.   ---Vance Bourjaily

•••

ANCESTORS

If you could see your ancestors
    All standing in a row,
I expect you would find there
    One or two you wouldn't care to know.
Because in climbing family trees
    One always meets a few
Who get there by irregular steps
    As such folks always do.
If you should meet your ancestors
    All standing in a row,
You would surely find there one or two
    Whom you would be proud to know.
But here's another question
    Which requires a different view.
If you should meet your ancestors
    Would they be proud of you?

•••

Every man is an omnibus in which his ancestors ride.

55

A great many prominent family trees were started by grafting.

...

You've got to do your own growing, no matter how tall your grandfather was.

...

Why Is It?
    Your ancestor's will leaves his estate to his
    beloved wife and children but doesn't name them?

...

A Long Will:
    Showman P.T. Barnum wrote a will fifty-three pages
    long and then had it published in book form.

...

It has been a continuing source of wonder and amusement that William Shakespeare's only bequest to his wife was his second-best bed.

...

To our grandchildren, what we tell them about their parents' childhood and our own young years is living history.   ---Ruth Goode

...

GRANDMOTHER'S OLD ARMCHAIR

My grandmother, she, at the age of eighty-three,
  One day in May was taken ill and died:
And after she was dead, the will of course was
  read
By a lawyer as we all stood side by side.
To my brother, it was found, she had left a hundred
  pound.
The same unto my sister, I declare;
  But when it came to me the lawyer said, "I see
She has left to you her old armchair."

Chorus:
        How they tittered, how they chaffed,
        How my brother and my sisters laughed,
        When they heard the lawyer declare
        Granny'd only left to me her old armchair.

I thought it hardly fair, still I said I did not care,
  And in the evening took the chair away.
My brother at me laughed, the lawyer at me chaffed,
  And said, "It will come useful, John, some day.
When you settle down in life,
  Find some girl to be your wife,
You'll find it very handy, I declare,
  On a cold and frosty night,
When the fire is burning bright.
  You can sit in your old armchair."

What the lawyer said was true.
  For in a year or two,   cont'd

57

cont'd

Strange to say, I settled down in married life.
  I first a girl did court and then a ring I bought,
Took her to the church, and then she was my wife.
  Now the dear girl and me
Are happy as can be.
  And when my work is done, I declare,
I ne'er abroad would roam.
  But each night I'd stay at home,
And be seated in my old armchair.

One night the chair fell down,
  When I picked it up I found
The seat had fallen out upon the floor,
  And there before my eyes
I saw to my surprise
  A lot of notes, ten thousand pounds or more.
When my brother heard of this
  The poor fellow, I confess,
Went nearly wild with rage and tore his hair.
  But I only laughed at him,
And I said unto him: "Jim,
  Don't you wish you had the old armchair?"

Chorus:
        No more they tittered, no more they chaffed.
        No more my brother and sisters laughed,
        When they heard the lawyer declare
        Granny'd only left to me her old armchair.
                            ---Composer Unknown

                    ...

58

It's what you listen to when you're growing up that you always come back to.   ---Al Cohen

. . .

We always believe those who resemble us.
                    ---Jean De La Fontaine

. . .

When I was younger, I could remember anything, whether it happened or not.   ---Mark Twain

. . .

The linking of the generations, the historical lineage of family, the sharing of love . . . give purpose to life.   ---Dr. George Landberg

. . .

They say genes skip generations. Maybe that's why grandparents find their grandchildren so likeable.

. . .

GENEALOGIST: One who traces back your family as far as your money will go.   ---Oscar Wilde

. . .

HOBBY: Hard work you wouldn't do for a living.

59

He walks as if balancing the family tree on his nose.
                              ---Raymond Moley

                    •••

If the very old will remember, the very young will
listen.   ---Chief Dan George

                    •••

Another year of climbing the genealogy tree.
I've looked under the leaves and what do I see?
You coming up, while I'm going down,
We compare notes on what we have found.
At times it's not much, just one name or two,
It's better than nothing, I know it's true.
Still we search on, through films and a book,
Hoping that our family's in the next one we look.
May next year be fruitful, our lost one we find,
And soon that our families will be intertwined.
I ask Santa to send us to all the right places,
To guide us and lead us, and to see smiling faces.
May each of you find your lost pioneer,
I wish you Merry Christmas and a Happy New Year!
                              ---Johann Pierce Long

                    •••

Take notes on the spot, a note is worth a cart-load of
recollections.   ---Ralph Waldo Emerson

                    •••

                    60

My folks didn't come over on the Mayflower, but they
were there to meet the boat.   ---Will Rogers

. . .

The man who boasts only of his ancestors confesses that
he belongs to a family that is better dead than alive.

. . .

Whoever serves his country well has no need of
ancestors.   ---Voltaire

. . .

A man can't very well make for himself a place in the
sun if he keeps continually taking refuge under the
family tree.

. . .

Remember, remember always, that all of us,
and you and I especially, are descended
from immigrants and revolutionists.
                    ---Franklin D. Roosevelt

. . .

Some men wake up to find themselves famous; others stay
up all night and become notorious.

. . .

61

                    The Body
                      of
            Benjamin Franklin, Printer
           (Like the cover of an old book,
                Its contents torn out,
        And stript of its lettering and gilding)
               Lies food for worms.
          Yet the work itself shall not be lost,
       For it will (as he believed) appear once more,
                   In a new
              And more beautiful edition,
                Corrected and amended
                      by
                  The Author
                       ---Benjamin Franklin

                      ...

Get your facts first, and then you can distort them as
much as you please.   ---Mark Twain

                      ...

   Never say you know a man until you have divided an
   inheritance with him.   ---Johann Caspar Lavater

                      ...

Greatness of name in the father ofttimes overwhelms the
son; they stand too near one another. The shadow kills
the growth.   ---Ben Jonson

                      ...

                      62

TO MY ANCESTORS

I see you toiling down the tedious years,
You bearded, gaunt, and bent old pioneers,
Sowing, and reaping, sowing once again,
In patience for an unborn race of men.

I see you struggling in the wilderness
Where failure meant starvation - and success
A cabin in the wilderness, rough hewn, crude,
Garments of homespun and the humblest food.

Tradition scarcely tells me whence you came,
I only know a few of you by name:
I only know you lived and multiplied
Quite profligate in progeny - and died.

Yet in my heart I know that most of you,
Were strong and steadfast and that one or two
At least had weaknesses that still may be
Traced in the trends of atavistic me.

One I am sure was blest with native wit -
I'm thankful he transmitted some of it! -
That helped him dodge Dame Trouble's swiftest dart,
And meet misfortune with a merry heart.

One was rather a worthless wight I fear,
Who when the bluebird whispered Spring was near
Forsook his plow - a shiftless sluggard one
And roamed the woods alone with rod and gun.

cont'd

63

And one a gentle dreamer was, I know,
Who, lured by shadows, let the substance go.
Twas he who dared the raging Western sea -
I'm glad he handed down his dreams to me!
                              ---"Eolus", Chicago Tribune

...

Snobs talk as if they had begotten their own ancestors.
                              ---Herbert Agar

...

There is something about a closet that makes a skeleton
terribly restless.   ---Wilson Mizner

...

                 Melchoir Leichtenstenkengstiger
              (An early resident of South Carolina)

...

The early North American Indian made a great mistake by
not having an immigration bureau.

...

Eulogy -
     Praise of a person who has either the advantages of
     wealth and power or the consideration to be dead.
                              ---Ambrose Bierce

...

A GENEALOGIST'S CHRISTMAS EVE

'Twas the night before Christmas
When all through the house
Not a creature was stirring,
Not even my spouse.

The dining room table with clutter was spread
With pedigree charts and with letters which said...
"Too bad about the data for which you wrote
Sank in a storm on an ill-fated boat."

Stacks of old copies of wills and the such
Were proof that my work had become much too much.
Our children were nestled all snug in their beds,
While visions of sugarplums danced in their heads.

And I at my table was ready to drop
From work on my album with photos to crop.
Christmas was here, and of such was my lot
That presents and goodies and toys I'd forgot.

Had I not been so busy with grandparents' wills,
I'd not have forgotten to shop for such thrills.
While others had bought gifts that would bring Christmas
cheers,
I'd spent time researching those birthdates and years.

While I was thus musing about my sad plight,
A strange noise on the lawn gave me such a great fright.
Away to the window I flew in a flash,
Tore open the drapes and I yanked up the sash.

65

THE SUNNY SIDE OF GENEALOGY

When what to my wondering eyes should appear,
But an overstuffed sleigh and eight small reindeer.
Up to the housetop the reindeer they flew,
With a sleigh full of toys and 'ole Santa Claus, too.

And then in a twinkle, I heard on the roof
The prancing and pawing of thirty-two hoofs.
As I drew in my head, and bumped it on the sash,
Down the cold chimney fell Santa - KER-RASH!

"Dear" Santa had come from the roof in a wreck,
And tracked soot on the carpet, (I could wring his short
neck!)
Spotting my face, good old Santa could see
I had no Christmas spirit you'd have to agree.

He spoke not a word, but went straight to his work
And filled all the stockings, (I felt like a jerk).
Here was Santa, who'd brought us such gladness and joy;
When I'd been too busy for even one toy.

He spied my research on the table all spread
"A genealogist!" He cried! (My face was all red!)
Tonight I've met many like you, Santa grinned.
As he pulled from his sack a large book he had penned.

I gazed with amazement - the cover it read
Genealogy Lines for Which You Have Plead.
"I know what it's like as a genealogy bug."
He said as he gave me a great Santa hug.

"While the elves make the sleighful of toys I now carry,

I do some research in the North Pole Library!
A special treat I am thus able to bring,
To genealogy folks who can't find a thing."

"Now off you go to your bed for a rest,
I'll clean up the house from this genealogy mess."
As I climbed up the stairs full of gladness and glee,
I looked back at Santa who'd brought much to me.

While settling in bed, I heard Santa's clear whistle,
To his team, which then rose like the down of a thistle.
And I heard him exclaim as he flew out of sight,
"Family History is Fun! Merry Christmas! Goodnight!"
                                    ---Author Unknown

···

The rarest quality in an epitaph is truth. ---Thoreau

···

Why Is It?
    The only overturned, face-down gravestone in the
    cemetery is your grandfather's?

···

What an enormous magnifier is tradition! How a thing
grows in the human memory and in the human imagination,
when love, worship, and all that lies in the human
heart, is there to encourage it.   ---Thomas Carlyle

···

GENEALOGIST'S POX

WARNING: Very contagious to adults.

SYMPTOMS: Continual complaint as to need for names,
dates and places. Patient has a blank expression,
sometimes deaf to spouse and children. Has no taste for
work of any kind, except feverishly looking through
records at libraries and courthouses. Has compulsion to
write letters. Swears at mailman when he doesn't leave
mail. Frequents strange places such as cemeteries;
ruins; and remote, desolate country areas. Makes secret
night calls, hides phone bills from spouse and mumbles
to self. Has a strange, faraway look in eyes.

NO KNOWN CURE.

TREATMENT: Medication is useless. Disease is not fatal,
but gets progressively worse. Patient should attend
genealogy workshops, subscribe to genealogical magazines
and be given a quiet corner in the house where he or she
can be alone.

REMARKS: The unusual nature of this disease is---the
sicker the patient gets, the more he or she enjoys it!

...

Why Is It?
    The person next to you has all the luck and you
    can't find a thing?

...   \

EPITAPH: A belated advertisement for a line of goods
that has been permanently discontinued. ---Irvin S. Cobb

. . .

> He first deceased;
> She for a little tried
> To live without him,
> Liked it not,
> And died.
> ---Sir Henry Wotton

. . .

That our children may be patriots, we tell them of their
fathers.   ---Benjamin Brink

. . .

Marriage Record in Shelby Co., Tenn:
    Bernard M. Patterson to Martha E. Bosley, Oct. 25,
    1848. (Note on marriage bond: "Dear Sir: You will
    oblidge me verry much if you do not mention my
    getting mariag licince from you on yesterday as some
    things have transpired that make it allmost
    impossible for me to attempt to consumate the
    matter. Your friend -- B.M. Patterson."

. . .

Gentility is what is left over from rich ancestors after
the money is gone.   ---John Ciardi

Notations written by doctors on Death Certificates:

"A mother died in infancy."
"Deceased had never been fatally sick."
"Died suddenly, nothing serious."
"Died suddenly at the age of 103."
"Went to bed feeling well, but woke up dead."
"Kicked by horse shod on left kidney."
"Pulmonary hemorrhage, sudden death. Duration four
      years."
"Deceased died from blood poison, caused by a broken
      ankle, which is remarkable, as the automobile
      struck him between the lamp and the radiator."

...

Reading the epitaphs, our only salvation lies in
resurrecting the dead and burying the living.
                                        ---Paul Eldridge

...

Epitaph:
                    Here Lyes Buried the
              Body of EBENEZER ALLEN, Efqr.
                        Who Died
                    May the 14th 1733:
                    In the 62D Year of
                        His Age
                  A Lover of Hospitality

...

THOUGHTS ON LINEAGE RESEARCH
by Prudence Groff Michael

My grandpa was the nicest man
Who ever drew a breath of air;
He came from good and simple folks
Whose lives were bright and fair....

And they, in turn, descended from
Identically the same.
Well-bred and ordinary type
Of gentleman and dame.

No trace of scandal ever touched
My grandpa or his kin....
Nor sordid, underhanded deeds
Were they included in:

Each lived--then passed to his reward
Within the starry skies....
And not a single bit of sin
Had EVER touched their lives.

But constantly I wish there had
For I'm left in the lurch....
And records on some nasty folks
Would surely help my research.

. . .

He who boasts of his descent praises the deeds of
another.   ---Seneca

71

While I have lived, I have striven to live worthily.
                                          ---Alfred

                        •••

            Whilst thy father lives
            Study his wishes;
            After he is dead
            Study his life.
                    ---Confucious

                        •••

A Will:
    The will of Frank C. Likas, probated April 26,
    1955, was written on a paper doily at a table in
    an Oak Lawn, Illinois restaurant.

                        •••

Why Is It?
    The information you desperately need could be found
    only on the 1890 census?

                        •••

Look not mournfully into the Past. It comes not back
again. Wisely improve the Present. It is thine.
                    ---Henry Wadsworth Longfellow

                        •••

        Life is the childhood of our immortality.

ON BEING AN ANCESTRESS
(To My Great-great Grandchildren)

I shall not care for it, I'm sure,
    The being dead, you know, my dears,
And hanging primly on a wall---
    Just looking on for years and years!

Ah, no, I'm sure I shall not like
    To be imprisoned there in paint;
I, who love being up-to-date,
    Shall never like just being - quaint!

Of course I'll do the proper thing,
    And hang serenely in my place
Beside your great-great grandpapa---
    A wifely smile upon my face!

And you will all look up to me---
    Believe, no doubt, I was a saint,
For all my faults, of course, will be
    Quite blotted out by time and paint!

No doubt your honored parents, dears,
    Will point my portrait out and say:
"Your great-great granny would be shocked---
    Things were so different in her day!"

And I'll not say a word, nor smile---
    I'll look demure, show no surprise---
But, dears, if you seek sympathy,
    I think you'll find it in my eyes!

73

> And if you stand and look at me,
>   And, wistful, wonder if I knew
> The pain, the passion and the stress
>   Of life, as they are felt by you,
>
> Come closer, dears, and never tell---
>   To you a secret I'll entrust:
> Your flaming hearts have caught their fire
>   From your great-great grandmother's dust!
>   ---Author Unknown

• • •

Birth, ancestry, and that which you yourself have not achieved can hardly be called your own.
                        ---Greek proverb

• • •

If men could see the epitaphs their friends write they would believe they had got into the wrong grave.
                        ---American proverb

• • •

A will is wealth's last caprice. ---Edward Bulwer-Lytton

• • •

A Verrrrry Long Name:
    Lake Chargoggagoggmanchauggagoggchaubunagungamaugg -
    a lake in Webster, Massachusetts.

• • •

74

YOUR NAME

You got it from your father
It was all he had to give
So it's yours to use and cherish
For as long as you may live.

If you lose the watch he gave you,
It can always be replaced
But a black mark on your name, Son,
Can never be erased.

It was clean the day you took it
And a worthy name to bear
When he got it from his father,
There was no dishonor there.

So make sure you guard it wisely,
After all is said and done
You'll be glad the name is spotless
When you give it to your son.

...

The will of the dead actor requested that his body be
cremated and ten per cent of his ashes thrown in his
agent's face.

...

A multitude of books distracts the mind.
---Seneca

ANCESTORS
by Bob Adams

Tell me lady, tell me sir,
    from what land your fathers were.

Very likely much like mine,
    many English in the line,
Drop of Irish, pinch of Scot,
    quite a bit of God knows what.

Little German, way on back,
    lots of Dutch along the track,
Or a warming wave by chance
    from the singing land of France.

Does another southern strain,
    rule your body and your brain,
With a dark Italian flood,
    or the surge of Israel's blood?

Deeply in the past we're rooted,
    not a race is undiluted;
Somewhere all of us have got
    quite a trace of God knows what.

Boast not your ancestral line
    and its record old and fine.
Mind the creed the peasants sung
    while democracy was young.

cont'd

cont'd

> "When Adam delved and Eve spun
>   who then was the gentleman?"
> Broadcast was the human seedling,
>   all the nations interbreeding.
>
> Merry gypsies, roaming free
>   set their marks on you and me,
> And the sons of conquering Rome
>   doubtless made themselves at home.
>
> Even though some sources were
>   what they call "bar sinister",
> We should thank the Lord a lot
>   for our strains of God knows what.

...

Some men's names appear in the paper only three times:
when they're too young to read, when they're too dazed
to read, and when they're too dead to read.

...

Every man is his own ancestor, and every man his own
heir. He devises his own future, and he inherits his
own past.   ---H.F. Hedge

...

Every man is a quotation from all his ancestors.

77

What's Your Name?   Silence Bellows
                     Safety First
                     Green Clay
                     Leen Hamm
                     Major Minor
                     Dr. Wagy, veterinarian
                     Mr. Bones, undertaker

...

CARTOON:
    Bank teller to man cashing a check: "Aside from your
    family coat of arms, do you have any other identifi-
    cation?"

...

Marriage is the root of every genealogical tree.
                                    ---Clemens

...

Many a tombstone is a grave error.

...

Permission to Marry in Champaign Co., IL:
            "Let him have the License. Yours in Sorrow"
                                    ---Martin Rinehart

...

Every family tree has its squirrels.

Epitaph:
Here lies the body of
Harry Hershfield
If not, notify
Ginsberg & Co. Undertakers,
at once

...

History is a pact between the dead, the living, and the
yet unborn.   ---Edmund Burke

...

Today's Chuckle:
If tombstones told the truth,
everyone would want to buried at sea.

...

I search for an ancestor with the family name
Who in history had some claim to fame.
I'd like to find someone who was great,
One whose actions I'd be proud to relate.
Alas, it's true - not one can I find
Who made a contribution to mankind.
Then I wonder if, in some future year
Another searches for someone to revere,
And finds my name on the family tree
Will he or she be proud to claim me.
                              ---Jack W. Briscoe

79

> The family of fools is ancient.
> ---Benjamin Franklin "Poor Richards Almanac"

...

OUR BELOVED KIN
by John V. Kirby

Climbing up your Family Tree
Is known as Gen-ea-logy
Now in your Family Tree you'll find
Kin of almost every kind

Some you'll love and some you'll hate
And wonder why by some cruel fate
They climbed into your Family Tree
But there they are for all to see

But as we work toward that dim past
Our kinfolks fade away at last
The farther back we try to go
The problems always seem to grow

Records seem to fade away
And proof is replaced by mere hearsay
But we keep on trying and now and then
We all come up with quite a gem

And feel our work has been worthwhile
And so we re-arrange our file
And ponder what next step to take
And what next journey we should make (cont'd)

80

(cont'd)

> So on we go with hopes anew
> Always looking for some clue
> To fill out gaps in previous work
> With a firm resolve that we won't shirk
> To solve all problems that we may meet
> To make our History all complete

...

Bob Brandon went to his 1940 high school reunion and found that he was listed as "deceased" on the program.

An award was later presented to the person in attendance who came the farthest. "I object", Brandon roared, waving the program. "I came back from the dead, and that's a lot further than Seattle!"

The committee overruled his objection.

---"The Blade", Toledo, OH

...

Supposedly an 1848 Epitaph in Paris, VA:
> Here lies:
> Two grandmothers, with their two grandaughters;
> Two fathers, with their two wives;
> Two mothers, with their two sons;
> Two sisters, with their two brothers;
> Yet but six corpses in all lie buried here,
> All born legitimate, from incest clear.

...

A Will:

A woman-hating man named T.M. Zink provided
that his $40,000 to $80,000 estate should go
into a trust fund for 75 years. At that time
the accumulated interest would bring the estate
up to $3,000,000, to be used for building a
womanless library named for himself. The words
"No Woman Admitted" must be cut in stone over
the main entrance of the library; only books by
men will be allowed; magazines will be censored
to eliminate articles by women. Nothing in the
design, decoration, or appointments of the
library must suggest feminine influence. The
will left $5 to his daughter and provides that
his widow is to have the use of the house as
long as she desires it for $40 a month rent.

---"Stories in Stone" by Charles L. Wallis

· · ·

SHOE by Mofnelly:
(1) "Doing a little research there, Skyler?..."
    "Yeah, I've been checking on our family tree..."
(2) "What did you find?"
(3) "A lot of root rot."

· · ·

BUMPERSTICKER:
Happiness is growing a family tree.

· · ·

Now that I have a computer for my genealogical records, I find that my records are just as confused as before, however, now my confusion is better organized.
                                        ---Jack W. Briscoe

• • •

There were human beings aboard the Mayflower, not merely ancestors.
                                        ---Stephen Vincent Benet

• • •

CARTOON:
        Woman looking at a tombstone:
        "I just knew she married that old goat!"

• • •

You can boast about anything if it's all you have. Maybe the less you have, the more you are required to boast.   ---"East of Eden" by John Steinbeck

• • •

EPITAPH: A memorial that usually lies above about the one that lies below.

• • •

BUMPERSTICKER:
        Do You Know Where Your Ancestors Are?

Ancestors are the people that made us possible.

•••

People are what they are because they have come out of
what was.   ---Carl Sandburg

•••

To know where I come from is one of the greatest
longings of the human heart. More than genealogical
data, we seek in the lives of those who went before us
the meaning of our lives.   ---Ardis Whitman

•••

It is absurd to think that life begins for us at birth.
The pattern was set far back; we merely step into the
process.   ---Kathleen Coyle

•••

This country needs a family tree producing more lumber
and fewer nuts.

•••

        Family trees are like most hedges -
        They have wild sprouts around the edges.

•••

SURNAME
by Janet M. Kendig

Have you ever met someone new
And when you got around to names
Discovered to your delight
Your name and theirs was the same?

You say, "We must be related!"
They say, "Oh, I doubt there is a way."
But if you do family research
That's one thing you NEVER say.

Almost everyone with the same surname
Is related in some form or other
It may take generations to prove it
It's obvious we are not brothers.

But even a cousin several times removed
Is a relative never-the-less
And I cherish every cousin I find
I know you are one of the best.

...

A Birthday Card:

(1) I'm glad we're related...
(2) I don't have to make excuses for being
     seen with you!

...

85

At a genealogical society meeting, an English woman
was telling about her search for ancestors who had
immigrated to America long ago. She informed the group
that the Americans had dropped a "t" from the spelling
of the family name. "I <u>know</u> they were my relatives,"
she summed up, "but what <u>did</u> they do with the 't'?"
From the side of the room came an unmistakable
Yankee drawl: "Why, didn't you know, ma'am? They dumped
<u>that</u> overboard at Boston!"

"Life in These United States", Reader's Digest.

•••

Do not resent growing old - many are denied that
privilege.

•••

A man's character is like a fence;
It cannot be strengthened by white wash.

•••

Life is a grindstone - whether it grinds you down or
polishes you up depends on what you're made of.

•••

Genealogy is like potato salad -
When you share it with others, it's a picnic.

•••

Why Is It?
    You finally find your ancestor's obituary in an old newspaper and all it says is "Died last week".

...

SMILE! It's library day!

...

BAKED ON A STONE

The following notice appeared in an English newspaper almost a century ago:
"There has been much alarm caused at Reading. It arose in this way. One lady discovered a skull and crossbones faintly but distinctly printed on her quartern loaf of bread. Another found 'Resurgam' on hers. Finally, one in the bloom of youth and health got a loaf of bread with 'Died on the 20th of September' on it, and she concluded at once she had only a short time to live. She would, perhaps, have brought about the fulfillment of the prophecy by dying of fright, had not the cause of these warnings been discovered. The baker's oven wanted fresh bottoming, and he had very improperly applied some old tablets in a disused churchyard for that purpose. Though nicely polished by the wear of years, they had retained enough of their inscriptions to give some faint impressions to the bread, and some very strong ones to the purchasers."

...

God is the only interpreter of epitaphs.

...

People are a good deal like trees. Those who make the
most bows do not often bear the most fruit.

...

The London Graphic newspaper announced the birth of
"three young children".

...

CARTOON:
   (One referee to another about an irate basketball
   coach) "His hobby must be genealogy...he thinks he
   knows the ancestry of every referee in the league".

...

ATTRIBUTES OF A GENEALOGIST

A good genealogist has an innate pride in family and
country, and recognizes his duty to search out and
record the truth. He becomes, first of all, a full-time
detective, a thorough historian, an inveterate snoop,
and at the same time, a confirmed diplomat, a keen
observer, a hardened skeptic, an apt biographer, a
qualified linguist, a part-time lawyer combined with
quite a lot of district attorney, a studious
sociologist, and --- above all, an accurate reporter.

88

PORTRAIT ON A WALL

Sometime when I have become
A quiet portrait on the wall
Will you, my fair descendant
Stop to think of me at all?

Suppose your hands are shaped like mine
And you have my keen sense of fun
Will there be one to tell you so --
Then, -- when my days are done?

If you love books and fires and songs,
And silver moons in velvet skies,
Toss me a look of shared delight
From those, my own dark eyes.

For there are kinships in a curl
And keepsakes in a spoken name;
The wine of life may yet be poured
By faded hands within a frame.

...

THE BORN LOSER - by Art Sansom
   (1) "Quit moping!"
   (2) "So you had your ancestry traced and it only
      goes back to 1911..."
   (3) "Why, I'll bet lots of people's ancestries
      probably only go, ha-ha, back, ha-ha, to, ha-
      ha-hahahahahaha..."

Genealogists are the only people I know
who read books back to front.

...

Here lies the body of our dead Anna
gone to death by a banana:
It wasn't the fruit that dealt the blow
But the skin of the thing that laid her low.
---Burlington.

...

CROCK by Rochin & Wilder
(1) "You might wonder what this book is, Foulet."
(2) "It's my family stump."
"Don't you mean family tree?"
(3) "Obviously you never met my relatives."

...

Like mother, like son.
He's a real fruit of the womb.

...

Brief epitaphs:
gardener: "Transplanted"
coalminer: "Gone underground for good"
author: "He has written finis"
painter: "A finished artist"
angler: "He's hooked it"

GENTLE FOLK
by Virginia Miner

It's nice to come from gentle folk
    Who wouldn't stoop to brawl,
Who never took a lusty poke
    At anyone at all.

Who never raised a raucous shout
    At any country inn
Or calmed an ugly fellow lout
    With a belaving pin,

Who never shot a revenuer
    Hunting for the still,
Who never rustled cattle, who're
    Pleased with uncle's will,

Who lived their lives out as thy ought,
    With no uncouth distractions,
And shunned like leprosy the thought
    Of taking legal actions.

It's nice to come from gentle folk
    Who've never known disgrace –
But oh, though scandal is no joke
    It's easier to trace!

. . .

Treat your family like friends
and your friends like family.

91

Epitaph in a New England cemetery:
   "I told you I was sick, Elizabeth."

...

Why Is It?
   You finally get a day off from work to travel to a
   courthouse - and when you get there it's closed for
   emergency plumbing repairs.

...

Before repeating anything "a little bird" told you,
better make sure it wasn't a little cuckoo.

...

   Behold the work of the Old...
   Let your Heritage not be lost,
   But bequeath it as a Memory,
   Treasure and Blessing...
   Gather the lost and the hidden
   And preserve it for thy Children.
                    ---Christian Metz.

...

FRANK AND ERNEST - by Thaves
   "During evolution, Ernie's ancestors were busy with
   something else."

...

92

WHICH ONE IS REALLY ME?
(Author Unknown)

I was once a normal person until
    I climbed the family tree,
Now that my ancestors have met
    they make a battle-ground of me.

My Grandpa Pat from Ireland
    makes me dance with lively feet;
While my English one - Sir Oliver -
    walks sedately down the street.

My Swedish Grandma Hilda gives
    away each dime I make,
While my Scottish one shudders
    at the things I waste and break.

My Great Grandma from Paris
    laughs and flirts the livelong day!
And my Great Grandma from Plymouth
    turns her back the other way.

Thus they argue - thus they differ,
    how I wish they would agree,
For I never can determine just
    which one is really me.

• • •

A man or woman is never truly dead, so long as a single
person has some knowledge or remembrance of them.

93

Birthday Card:
   (1)   Happy Birthday to a relative who's a credit to
         our family...
   (2)   And you know how hard it is to get credit in
         this family!

                        ...

Ivy Saunders' four husbands:
                  Here lie my husbands
                        1 - 2 - 3
                  As still as men
                  could ever be:
                  As for the fourth:
                  Praise be to God
                  He still abides
                  Above the sod:
                  Abel, Seth and Leidy
                  Were the first 3 names
                  And to make things tidy
                  I'll add his --- James

                        ...

                  WHO NEEDS ANCESTORS?
                  by Ruth Boorstin

                  To study genealogy
                  Is just not any fun:
               I'd rather own a good stock
               Than claim I came from one.
                        ---The Wall Street Journal

                        94

PLEA TO AN ANCESTOR
by Winston De Ville

Ancestor! Ancestor,
    Oh, why be elusive?
When all that I seek is of you
    proof conclusive?
Your birth date, the place, the
    time of your passing.
Your wedding, with whom?
    That's all I am asking.
I spy and I pry into family
    tradition.
Old letters I read - they're
    in awful condition!
Court records were burned in
    "The War" (as you know).
To graveyards in brambles
    and briers I oft' go.
So, somewhere and somehow,
    I'll find you one day,
With "preponderance of
    evidence", as we like to say.
Then, Eureka! Rejoice!
    I'll write me a book!
I'll cite all my sources,
    be you gentle - or crook.
So help me, do please;
    neither shy nor coy be.
If you were where 'twould
    help, I'd send an S.A.S.E.
       ...

95

FAMILY
by Janet M. Kendig

Families are groups of people
Who share names & habits & tastes
Each one has something of the other
But each is a brand new face.

He or she helps broaden the circle
That began generations ago
So you see we are all still family
Even though some we don't know.

Family Bibles tell the stories
of marriages, births & deaths
Books that are written about us
Help others to know us best.

But what really makes us a family?
It's the knowing that each one belongs;
That our roots are forever entwined,
And the family circle is strong.

...

GENEALOGISTS
by Roger C. Tripp

Well ancestors can be very intriguing folks,
When into their Bibles and crypts one pokes.
Their births and deaths and new generations,
Can give us all the utmost of frustrations.

96

Why couldn't they just have written it down,
Even a simple paragraph, sentence or noun.
But they were busy with children and such,
And have left it all for us to retouch.
But do we do justice to all of our kin?
Are we now finished or did we just begin?
Where were they born and where did they live?
Or has this escaped us like sand in a sieve?
Did they have money and live in big houses?
Or were they poor as proverbial church mouses?
Were they happy with laughter and glee?
Or was hurt and sorrow their real destiny?
It really does pain us not to have roots,
So we go on looking for genealogy recruits.
If you want to join us then give us some clues,
And start at whatever places you choose.
For our information is spotty at best,
And you might be the one to figure the rest.
So here's to good luck in finding your past,
It takes dedication, valor and being steadfast.
Now don't get depressed when you seem to be lost,
It is part of the journey and part of the cost.
But the rewards will certainly be worth the bother,
When stumbling upon your lost great-great-grandfather.
I'll pass on just one more tad of advice,
And you may well think this a bit overnice.
But in this good family we never permit,
Any children to be listed as illegitimate!

...

The best blood will sometimes get into a fool or a
mosquito.   ---Austin O'Malley

FAMILY REUNION
by Peg Meier

Where did I come from?
Who were my kin?
Why do I look like I do?
What are my talents?
When will I know
If I am related to you?

I've searched through the records
To learn what I can,
In libraries, courthouses, too.
Your name can't be found,
You weren't around,
Oh, why can't I find out about you?

The cards were all sent,
A reunion was held,
I came and I thought we would meet.
But you didn't show,
So how will I know,
That it is you,
When we pass on the street?

...

Names are not always what they seem.
The common Welsh name Bzjxxllwcp is pronounced Jackson.
---Mark Twain

...

98

LINES TO GRANNY
by Mary F. Kohlstrom

Where did you come from, Granny dear?
How did you get from there to here?
Tell me, what was your maiden name?
Has it always been spelled the same?
Where was your birthplace, county and state?
When were you born? Please give me the date.

(No, no, Granny, never you fear!
I'll put your birthday but NOT the year.
We'll leave that blank on the family tree;
I promise your secret won't go beyond me!)

Who was your father? Do you have proof?
What other children lived under his roof?
And what of your mother? Who was she?
What do you know of her pedigree?
When were they married? Can it be proved
That they were not cousins once removed?

I have a few questions to ask you still:
Did your father own land? Did he leave a will?
Your vital records, where are they?
What do ORIGINAL sources say?
We must have documents, one or two,
To prove, dear Granny, that you are you!

• • •

We are all citizens of history.

99

A nickname is the hardest stone that can be thrown at a genealogist.

•••

In 1839 a minister certified a marriage in Effingham County, Illinois, with the following poetry:

"On the eighteenth of April, at candlelight time,
In the year eighteen hundred and thirty-nine,
I joined in wedlock, during natural life,
The within Samuel Fuller and Polly, his wife.

The table, then sumptuously covered and spread,
For the guests, at which they heartily fed.
Great joy to the groom, and great joy to the bride,
Were the wishes of all, and God for their guide."

•••

Epitaph in Cambridge:
Here lies the body
of Mary Gwynne
who was so very
pure within
she cracked the shell
of her earthly skin
and hatched herself
a cherubim

•••

ADDITIONS

ADDITIONS